Dive in to KS2 Science with CGP!

This fantastic CGP book is a great way to help pupils strengthen their understanding of Year 5 Science.

It's packed with short bursts of practice at the perfect level for Year 5 pupils. There's a fun puzzle for every section, and we've even included pre-topic tests so you can check pupils' prior knowledge before they get stuck in.

We've included full answers to every question, and a handy progress chart to make marking a breeze!

What CGP is all about

Our sole aim here at CGP is to produce the highest quality books — carefully written, immaculately presented and dangerously close to being funny.

Then we work our socks off to get them out to you — at the cheapest possible prices.

Contents

Section 6 – Mixed Practice

Published by CGP

Editors: Katherine Faudemer, Rachel Hickman, Luke Molloy, Charlotte Sheridan
With thanks to Sarah Pattison and Kate Whitelock for the proofreading.
With thanks to Emily Smith for the copyright research.

ISBN: 978 1 78908 905 9
Clipart from Corel®
Illustrations by: Sandy Gardner Artist, email sandy@sandygardner.co.uk
Printed by Elanders Ltd, Newcastle upon Tyne.
Based on the classic CGP style created by Richard Parsons.

Getting Started

1. Name a habitat where you are likely to find a frog.

    ....

2. Flowering plants are pollinated to make seeds.

    a) Tick two ways that flowers can be pollinated.

    ☐ by insects   ☐ by eggs   ☐ by explosion   ☐ by wind

    b) What happens during seed dispersal?

    ....

    ....

3. Below are pictures of some animals.
    Circle the animals that don't lay eggs.

    Zebra

    Owl

    Mouse

    Duck

    Frog

    Dog

    Turtle

    Llama

Test 1 – Life Cycles

Warm up

1. Draw lines connecting each animal to its life cycle.

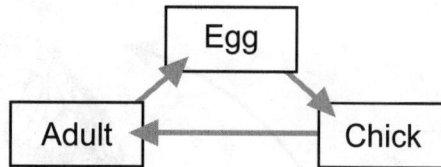

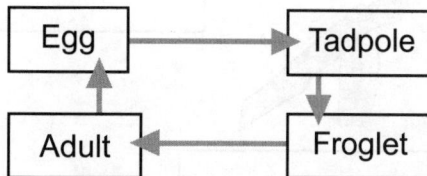

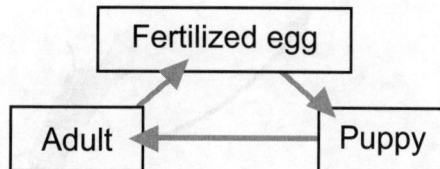

Egg → Chick → Adult → Egg

Egg → Tadpole → Froglet → Adult → Egg

Fertilized egg → Puppy → Adult → Fertilized egg

___
2 marks

2. Tick the two correct sentences below.

Most mammals hatch from eggs. ☐

Female mammals usually carry their developing offspring inside themselves. ☐

Most mammals form a chrysalis in order to change into an adult. ☐

Most female mammals give birth to live young. ☐

___
2 marks

3. Below is a diagram showing the life cycle of a butterfly.

    a) Use some of the words below to label the diagram.

    adult butterfly   **babies**   **eggs**   **worm**

    caterpillar   **lice**   **chrysalis**   **leaf**

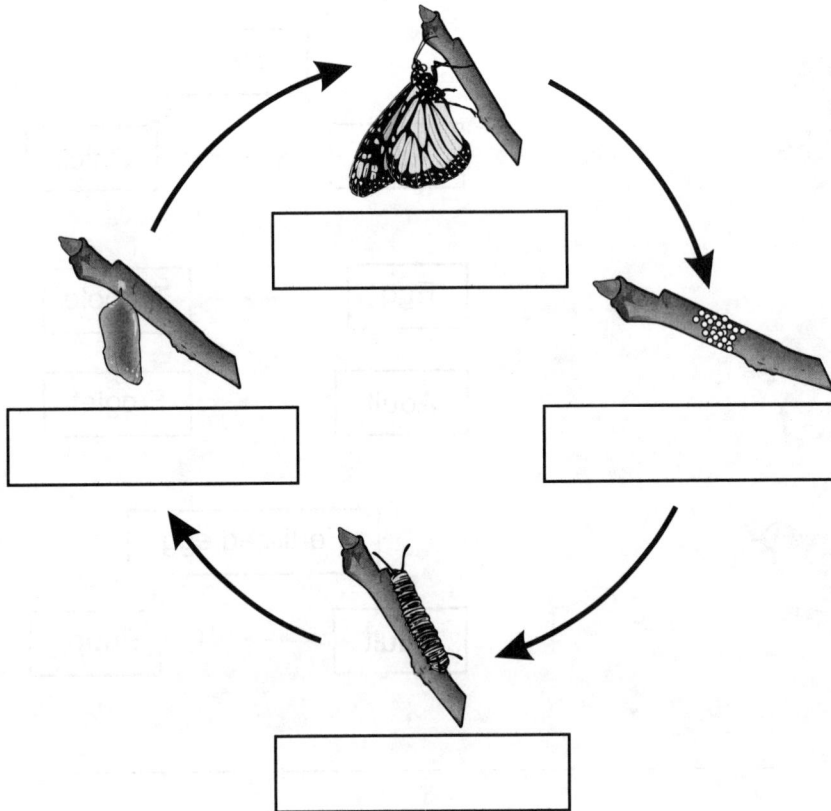

4 marks

    b) Give one difference between the life cycle of
        a butterfly and the life cycle of a bird.

    ....

1 mark

    c) Give one similarity between the life cycle of
        a butterfly and the life cycle of a frog.

    ....

1 mark

4. Use words from the list to answer the questions.
   You can use each word more than once.

   amphibians   **insects**   **birds**   **mammals**

   a) Which animals usually lay eggs as part of their life cycle?

   .... , ... and ....

   _____
   1 mark

   b) Which animals always lay their eggs in water?

   ....

   _____
   1 mark

   c) Which animals often go through a life cycle stage called 'pupa'
      or 'chrysalis' where they transform from a larva into their
      adult form?

   ....

   _____
   1 mark

5. The table below contains some unusual animals.
   Use your knowledge of birds, mammals, amphibians
   and insects to complete the last column.

Name of animal	Does it lay eggs?	Name of its young	What type of animal is it?
Aha Ha	Yes	larva	
Kagu	Yes	chick	
Golden Mantella	Yes	tadpole	
Fossa	No	cub	

   3 marks

   Score: / 16

Test 2 – Reproduction

Warm up

1. Most animals reproduce sexually.

   a) Circle the picture that shows the animals that can produce a lion cub through sexual reproduction.

   two female lions

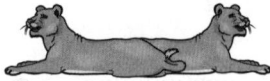

   a male and a female lion

   a female lion and
   a male cub

   three male lions _____

   1 mark

   b) Give one reason for your choice.

   ....

   ....

   1 mark

2. Circle the correct words to complete the sentences below.

   Some plants can reproduce without being **pollinated / pregnant**.

   Asexual / Sexual reproduction is when a new plant grows from

   small **petals / cuttings** of an old plant. Growing plants, such as

   daffodils, from **seeds / bulbs** is also asexual reproduction.

   _____

   3 marks

3. Baby animals are made by sexual reproduction.
   This is when an egg is fertilised by a sperm.

   a) Circle the animals below that produce sperm. Draw an X over
      the animals that produce eggs.

female horse

female dog

male cockerel

male orca

male snake

female bee

_____
2 marks

   b) The stages of sexual reproduction are given below but they
      are in the wrong order. Write the numbers 2-4 in the boxes to
      put the stages in order. The first one has been done for you.

The fertilised egg develops into an embryo.   ☐

The sperm joins with the egg, fertilising it.   ☐

The embryo continues to grow into a baby animal.   ☐

The sperm swims towards the egg.   1

_____
2 marks

4. The reproductive organs of a plant are inside the flower.

a) Use the words below to label this diagram of a flower.

filament   stigma   anther   ovary   style   petal

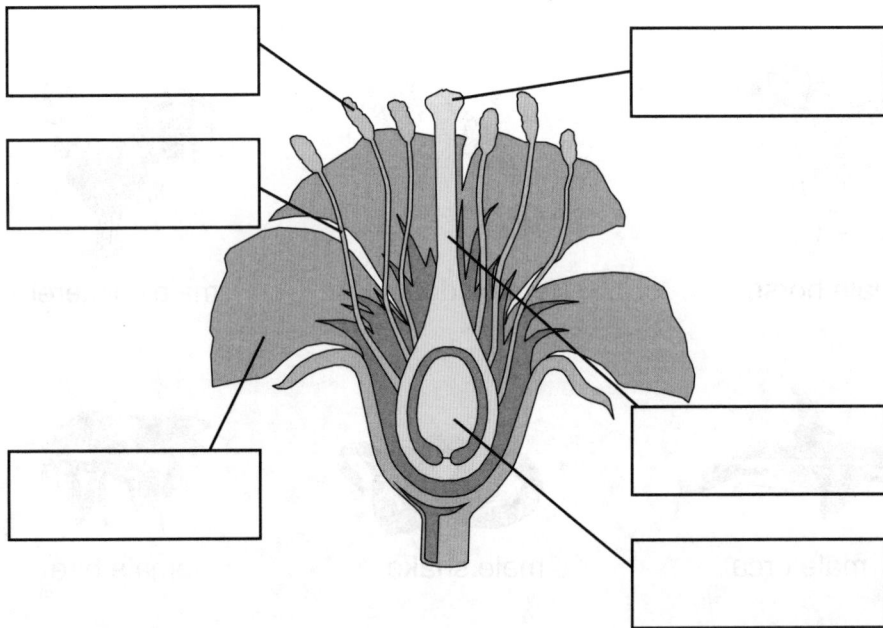

4 marks

b) Fill in the gaps in the sentences using some of the words below.

ovary   sperm   seed   stigma

egg   pollen   bulb

Pollination happens when .... from one plant

lands on the .... of another plant. Fertilisation

happens after pollination. This is when the pollen grain and the

.... join and this develops into a ....

3 marks

Score: / 16

Living Things Thinker

Use the clues to complete the crossword.
Then unscramble the letters in the shaded boxes to complete the sentence.

Down

1. This happens when pollen lands on the stigma of a plant.

2. This type of reproduction requires an egg to be fertilised.

3. Organisms can _____ sexually or asexually to produce offspring.

6. A life stage of an insect, sometimes called a grub.

Across

4. The name for all the stages that an organism goes through in its life. (Hint: it's two words.)

5. This type of reproduction happens when part of a plant grows into a new plant.

7. This happens when sperm or pollen join with an egg.

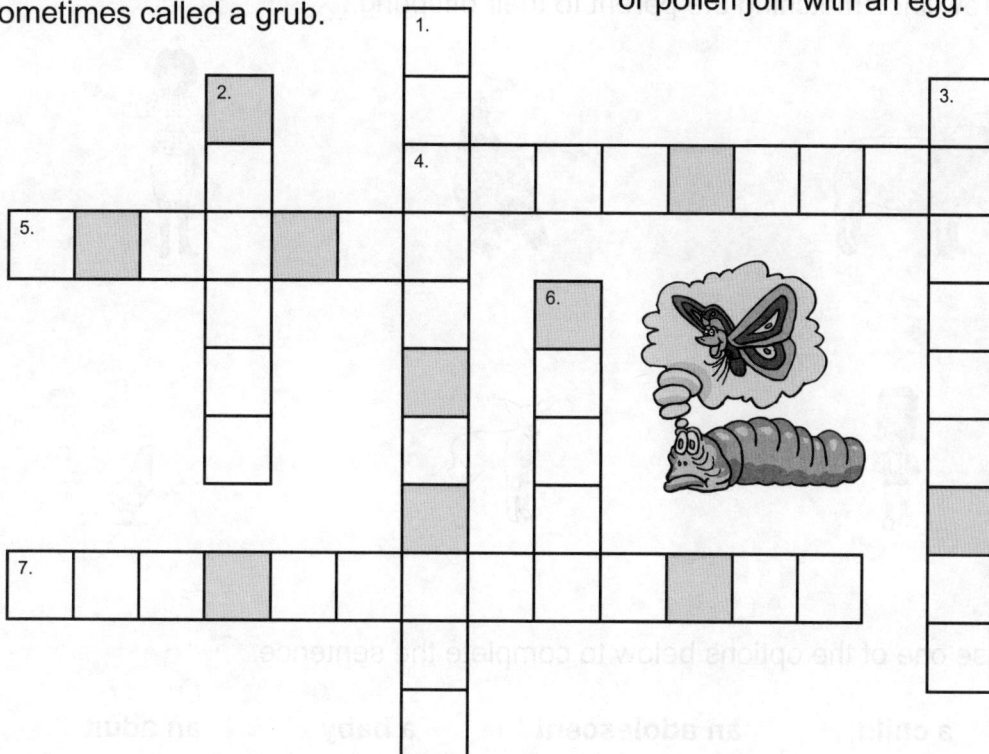

Asexual reproduction happens in plants when B ☐ ☐ B ☐

or ☐ ☐ ☐ ☐ ☐ ☐ G ☐ are planted in damp soil.

9

Getting Started

1. Label the people below from youngest to oldest, where 1 is the youngest and 3 is the oldest.

    ....

2. Draw lines matching the parent to their offspring.

3. Use one of the options below to complete the sentence.

    a child   **an adolescent**   **a baby**   **an adult**

    My teacher is ....

Test 1 – Human Growth

Warm up

1. Use the table to help you circle the two sentences that are true.

Animal	Gestation period (length of pregnancy)	Average weight of a newborn (kg)
Human	9 months	3.5
Elephant	22 months	100
Cat	2 months	0.1
Chimpanzee	8 months	1.8

Chimpanzees weigh more than humans when they are first born.

The gestation period of a cat is longer than that of a human.

Elephants are pregnant for more than a year longer than humans.

The gestation period of a human is 9 months.

_____
2 marks

2. Tick the boxes below to show whether each sentence is true or false.

True **False**

Humans stop growing taller when they reach adulthood.

Puberty happens during adolescence.

Humans get more dependent on their parents as they grow.

Adults become stronger when they reach old age.

_____
4 marks

11

Section 2 — Animals Including Humans

3.   Label each stage of the human life cycle in the diagram below.

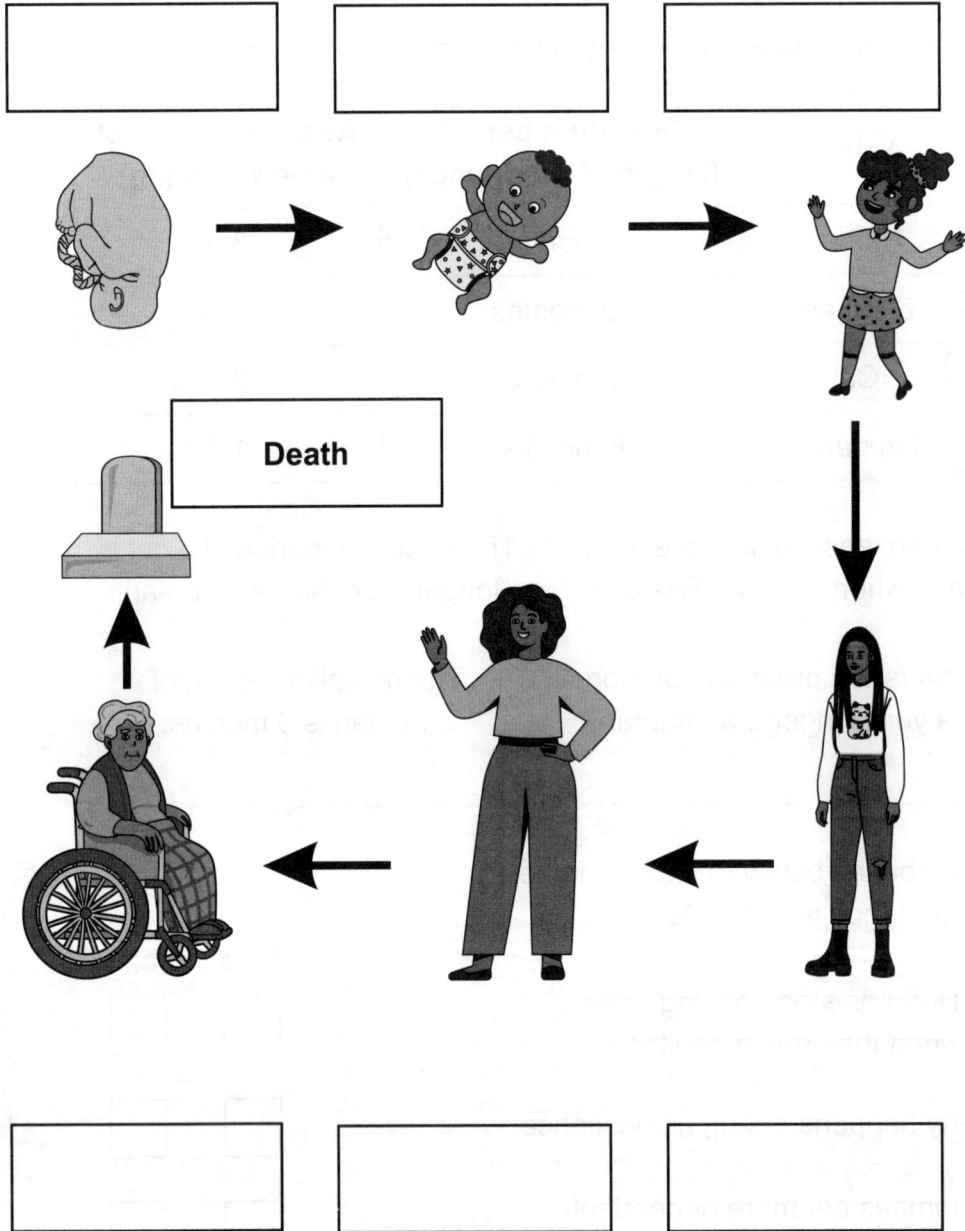

Death

4 marks

4. Both girls and boys go through puberty during adolescence. Lots of changes happen to them during that time.

a) Complete the table by ticking or crossing each box to show if each change happens to girls, to boys or to both girls and boys. The first row has been done for you.

Changes	Boys	Girls
Their testicles begin to produce sperm.	✔	✗
Their hips become wider.		
More oil is produced in their skin.		
Their voices become deeper.		
Hair starts to grow on their bodies.		

4 marks

b) List two more changes that girls experience during puberty.

1. ....

2. ....

2 marks

Score: _____ / 16

Unscramble to Escape

Follow the path through the room by filling in the answers to the clues.
Then unscramble the letters in the shaded squares to complete the sentence below.
The missing word will open the padlock and let you escape.

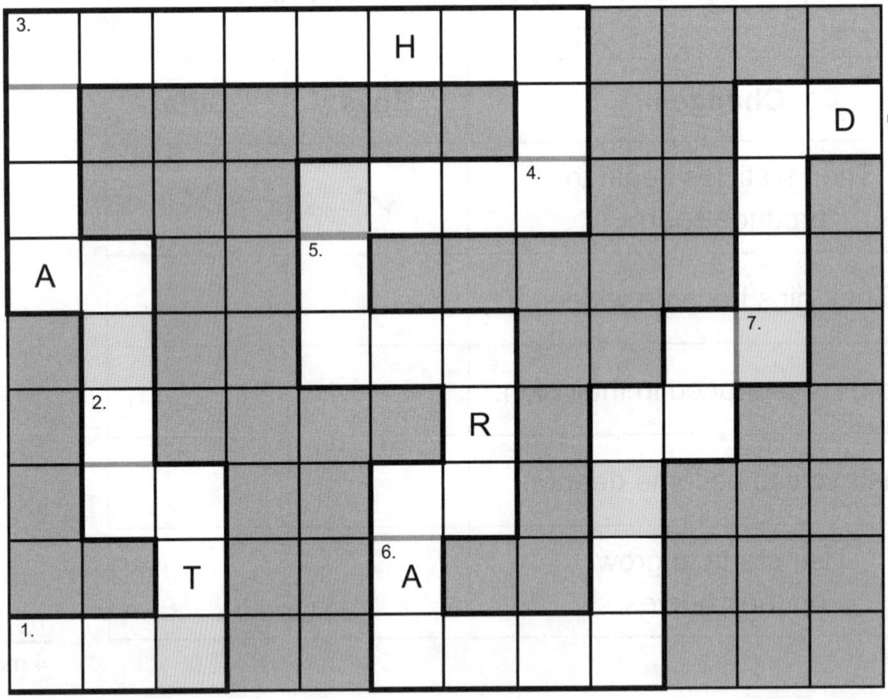

The crossword grid contains the following filled letters:

- 3. **H** (row 1)
- **D** (row 2)
- 4. (row 3)
- 5. (row 4)
- **A** (row 4)
- 7. (row 5)
- 2. **R** (row 6)
- **T** (row 8)
- 6. **A** (row 8)
- 1. (row 9)

1. Unscramble the life stage: **TFUOES**

2. The stage of life of a person over 65 years old.

3. The stage of life of a person aged 21.

4. [image of a baby]

5. The time during adolescence when the body changes and develops.

6. [image of a teenager]

7. A five year old is a _____.

During their lifetimes all living things go through changes.

These changes make up their life ....

Getting Started

1. Tick the sentence below that is correct.

   All materials are magnetic. ☐

   Only some metals are magnetic. ☐

   Fabric is magnetic. ☐

2. The diagram shows the states of matter of water.
   Complete the labels using the words below.

   melting   **freezing**   **evaporating**   **condensing**

   ....

   ice   water   steam

   ....

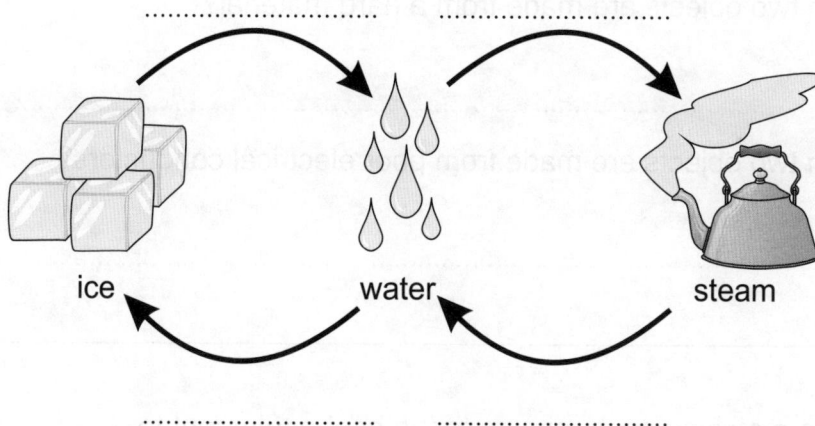

3. Circle the correct words to complete the sentences below.

   Electric wires are made from copper and are covered with plastic.

   Copper is a **good / poor** electrical conductor. Electricity can flow

   through it with **difficulty / ease**. Plastic is a **good / poor** electrical

   insulator, so it protects you from getting an electric shock.

⏱ 🔟 Test 1 – Material Properties and Changes

Warm up

1. Use the objects below to answer the questions.

 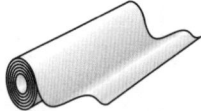  

steel screw   tin foil   plastic sandwich bag   wooden table

a) Which object is made from a transparent material?

....

1 mark

b) Which two objects are made from a hard material?

....

1 mark

c) Which two objects are made from poor electrical conductors?

....

1 mark

2. Draw lines matching each mixture to the best equipment to use to separate them. You can only use each method once.

sand and water   small-holed sieve

sand and iron filings   medium-holed sieve

flour and rice   filter paper

marbles and sand   magnet

2 marks

3. Freya stirs one teaspoon of salt into a glass of warm water.

a) What will happen to the salt? Circle the correct answer.

It will disappear.   It will float on top of the water.

It will sink to the bottom of the glass.   It will dissolve.

1 mark

b) Circle the correct word to complete the sentence.

Stirring salt into water creates a **mixture / solution**.

1 mark

c) How can Freya get the salt back? Tick the correct box.

Use filter paper to separate the salt and the water.

Evaporate off the water to leave the salt behind.

Freeze the water and the salt will come back.

1 mark

4. Kai put 200 ml of water at 70 °C into four identical cups wrapped in different materials. He waited five minutes, then measured the temperature of the water again and recorded it in the table.

Material	Temp. after 5 minutes
polystyrene	62 °C
cardboard	58 °C
aluminium foil	45 °C
thin plastic	53 °C

a) Which material was the best thermal conductor?

....

1 mark

b) Why might polystyrene make a good hot drinks cup?

....

....

....

2 marks

5. Materials can be changed and these changes
    can be reversible or irreversible.

    a) What is meant by a 'reversible change'?

        ....

        ....

        _____
        1 mark

    b) Circle the three reversible changes below.

    **melting an
    ice cube**   **frying an egg**   **dissolving
                                                             sugar in water**

    **burning
    a match**   **mixing vinegar and
                      bicarbonate of soda**   **mixing flour
                                                      and salt**
                                                      _____
                                                      2 marks

    c) Tick the two boxes that can correctly complete the sentence.

        Baking a cake is an irreversible change because...

            ...you cannot get the raw ingredients back.   ☐

            ...you can get the ingredients back again.   ☐

            ...a new and different material has been made.   ☐

            ...it is too complicated to reverse.   ☐
                                                                      _____
                                                                      2 marks

                                            Score: [   ] / 16

Material Mystery

Use the definitions to complete the words. Then unscramble the letters in the shaded boxes to reveal the mystery word.

The process where a gas cools and becomes a liquid.

⬜⬜⬜ D ⬜⬜⬜⬜⬜⬜⬜

A change where you can get the starting materials back.

⬜⬜⬜⬜⬜⬜⬜⬜⬜ E

The name of a process for separating a solid from a liquid.

F ⬜⬜⬜⬜⬜⬜⬜

What is formed when a solid dissolves in a liquid?

⬜⬜⬜ L ⬜⬜⬜⬜

The name for different materials mixed together.

⬜⬜ X ⬜⬜⬜⬜

A solid that dissolves in a liquid is _____.

⬜⬜⬜⬜ B ⬜⬜

⬜⬜ R ⬜⬜⬜⬜⬜⬜ B ⬜⬜

CLUE: The mystery word means something that cannot be undone.

19   Section 3 — Properties and Changes of Materials

Getting Started

1. Which three of these are planets?
   Circle the correct answers.

   Jupiter

   The Sun

   The Earth

   Neptune

   The Moon

2. Which two of these happen at sunrise?
   Tick the correct answers.

   The sky gets darker. ☐   It goes from night to day. ☐

   The sky gets lighter. ☐   It goes from day to night. ☐

3. There are many moons in the solar system.

   a) How many moons orbit the Earth?

   ....

   b) Complete the sentence by circling the correct option.

   Many **planets** / **stars** in the solar system have moons orbiting them.

Warm up

1. Complete the labels on the diagram to show which side of Earth is in day time and which is in night time.

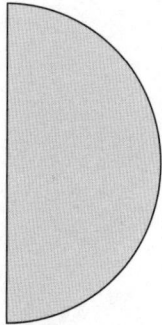 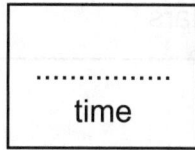  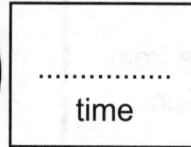

.... time   .... time

The Sun   Earth

_____
1 mark

2. What do all the planets in the solar system orbit?
   Tick the correct answer.

   ☐ Earth   ☐ The Moon   ☐ Mars   ☐ The Sun

   _____
   1 mark

3. Complete the sentences by using some of the words below.

South	rotating	East	orbiting	North	still	West

   As the day goes on, the Sun appears to move across the sky from

   .... to .... This happens because the

   Earth is ....

   _____
   3 marks

4. There are eight planets in our solar system.

   a) Write the missing planets in the boxes below, so
      that they are in order of their distance from the Sun.

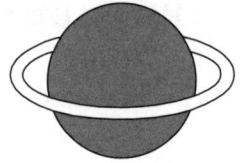

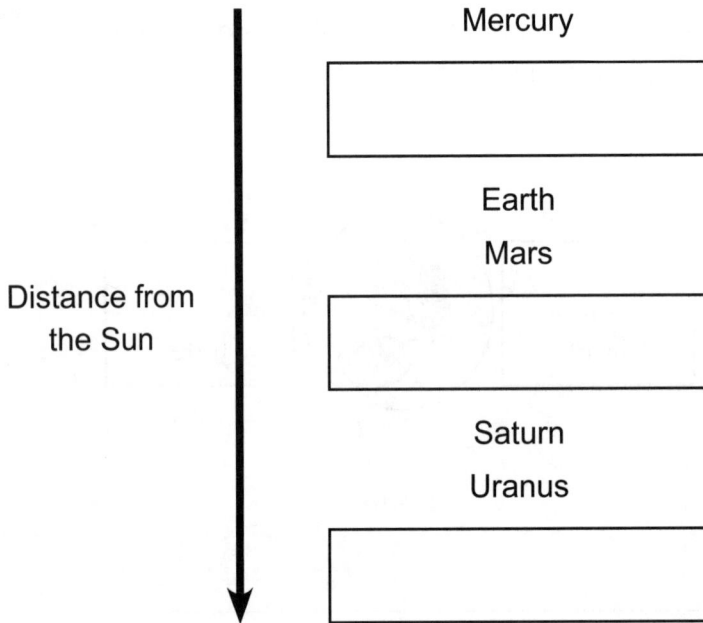

Mercury

| |
| |

Earth

Mars

Distance from
the Sun

| |
| |

Saturn

Uranus

| |
| |

3 marks

   b) What force keeps the planets in orbit?

   ....

1 mark

   c) The planets are all approximately what shape?
      Circle the correct option below.

   spherical   **triangular**   **circular**   **cylindrical**

1 mark

5. Some planets have moons.
   Tick whether the following statement is true or false.

                                         TRUE   **FALSE**

        The movement of Earth's   ☐   ☐
        moon causes day and night.

1 mark

6. Write the length of time each of these movements takes.

How long the Earth takes to
rotate once on its axis = ... hours

How long it takes the Moon
to orbit the Earth = ... days

How long it takes the Earth
to orbit the Sun = ... days

3 marks

7. The letters in the diagram below show four positions that the Moon can be in during its orbit.

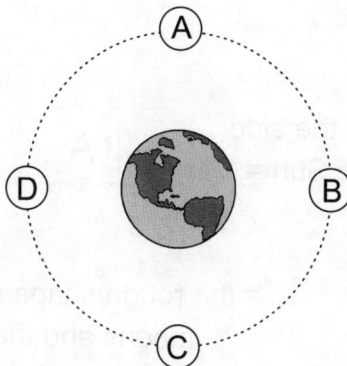

a) Which letter, A, B, C, or D, shows the position of a full moon?

....

1 mark

b) Describe why it's hard to see the Moon from Earth when it's in position D.

....

....

1 mark

Score: / 16

Solar System Search

Complete the key words using the definitions.
Use the letters in the grey boxes to answer the final question.

| | | O | | = a lump of rock that orbits a planet

the force that keeps
objects in orbit = | | | | | | | Y |

| | | A | | | | = what the Earth does on its own axis

The time of day for the side
of Earth facing the Sun = | | A | | | | |

| | P | | | | = the rough shape of planets,
moons and the Sun

the star at the centre of the solar system = | | | N |

| | | | E | | | = objects that orbit stars

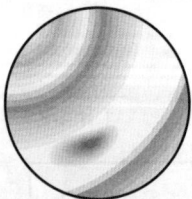

Each highlighted letter is the first letter of a planet in the solar system.
The first letter of one planet is missing. What is the planet?

....

Getting Started

1. Circle the examples where two objects need to be touching for the force to act.

Fridge magnets attracted by a force to a fridge.

A force bringing an apple down to the ground.

A woman using a force to kick a football.

A karate champion using a force to break a block.

A boy using a force to pull a sledge of gifts across snow.

A magnet using a force to pick up paper clips.

2. Pick one surface from the box that completes each sentence correctly.

| rough sandpaper | sand | polished metal | fairly smooth pavement |

The bottom of an ice skate should be made of ....

A cycle path should be made of ....

Test 1 – Forces

Warm up

1. Use the words in the box to fill in the sentences.

rough	pushes	air
water	smooth	pulls

Forces are always .... or ....

It's easier to pull an object across a .... surface

than a .... surface.

It's easier for a person to walk through ....

than ....

_____
3 marks

2. Tick the correct boxes to show whether each
of the objects will speed up or slow down.

	speed up	slow down
A bike rolling from a smooth road onto grass.	☐	☐
A go-kart being pushed by a friend.	☐	☐
A carrot dropped from the top turret of a castle.	☐	☐
A skydiver when she opens her parachute.	☐	☐

_____
2 marks

26

3. Draw lines to match the activities with the amount of friction needed.

**Skis sliding
on snow**

**As little friction
as possible**

**Car tyres rolling
on a road**

**As much friction
as possible**

**Holding onto a rock
when rock climbing**

**Some friction, but
not too much**

4. a) Tick the correct description of gravity on Earth.

    ☐ A force that only acts on falling objects.

    ☐ A force that pulls all objects towards the Earth's centre.

    ☐ A force that pushes all objects away from the Earth's centre.

    ☐ A force that pushes all objects towards the Earth's centre.

    b) Draw an arrow in each box below to show the direction in which the force of gravity is acting on the plane and on the skier.

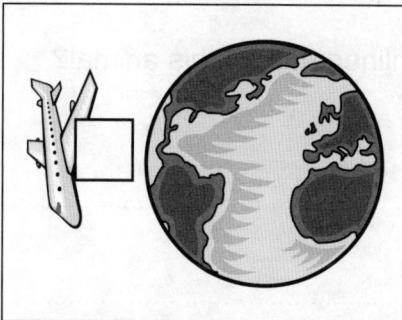

27

5. An object having a streamlined shape reduces the friction it experiences in air and water.

    a) Name the two types of friction that act on objects moving through air or water.

        ....

    b) Circle the vehicle below that is the most streamlined.

        Describe how the vehicle's shape makes it streamlined.

        ....

        ....

    c) Circle the animal below that is the most streamlined.

        sloth   **dolphin**

        What effect do you think being streamlined has on this animal? Explain your answer.

        ....

        ....

Score: / 15

Warm up

1. Adele is using mechanisms to help her in the garden.
    For each picture below, say whether the mechanism
    Adele is using is a lever, pulley or gear.

The mechanism is a ....

The mechanism is a ....

2 marks

2. The sentences below explain how a lever works, but they're in the wrong order.
    Write the letters A-D in the boxes to show the correct order.

    A: A small force is applied to the long side of the pole.

    B: A pole is placed on a pivot, with an object on the short side.

    C: A large force is produced on the short side of the pole.

    D: The pole moves on the pivot.

    ☐ → ☐ → ☐ → ☐

2 marks

3. Circle the four objects below that use a lever
    or a pulley to make the work easier.

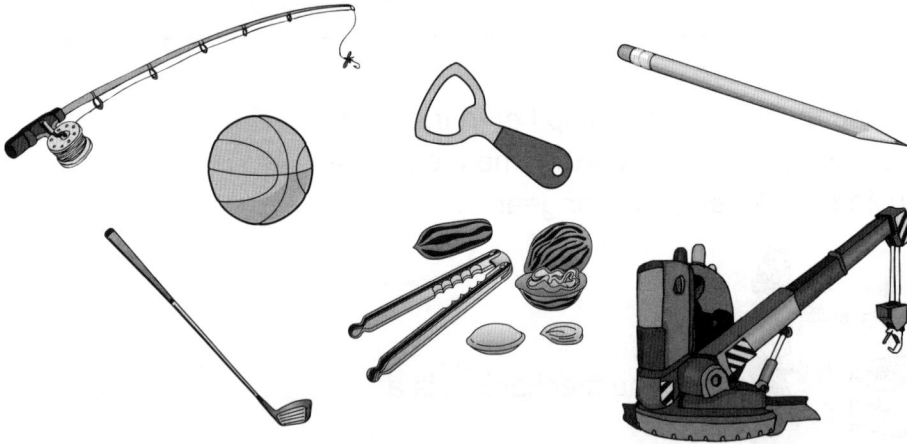

4 marks

4. Shane tries three different methods for lifting his school bag.

a) Which method would he find the hardest to lift the bag with?

    ....

1 mark

b) Describe one change he could make to method 3 that would
    make lifting the bag easier.

    ....

    ....

1 mark

5. Circle the correct words in the sentences below about clocks.

Clocks use **gears** / **pulleys** to turn the hour, minute and

second hands. The **ropes** / **cogs** connected to each

hand have a different number of **strings** / **teeth**, so they

turn **at different speeds** / **in different directions**.

_____
2 marks

6 a) Look at these pictures.

removing a nail

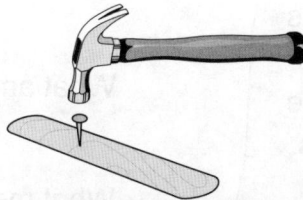
hammering in a nail

Which action involves the hammer being used as a lever?

....

_____
1 mark

b) Explain how this works.

....

....

....

_____
2 marks

Score: / 15

Mechanisms Riddles

Solve each riddle to work out what each item is.
Then work out whether the item uses levers, pulleys or gears.

1.

There's only one of me
but I'm called a pair.
Use me if you find
you've got too much hair.

What am I? ....

What mechanism do I use? ....

2.

I have hands
but no arms.
I have a face
but no eyes.

What am I? ....

What mechanism do I use? ....

3.

I'm found in cities,
often much taller
than the buildings.
I can move things
from place to place
whilst standing in one spot.

What am I? ....

What mechanism do I use? ....

4.

I go up at the
same time as
I go down.
You'll need
a friend to
use me in the
playground.

Riddle solver
On a seat
In a classroom
In a science lesson

What am I? ....

What mechanism do I use? ....

32

Test 1 – Mixed Test

(10)

Warm up

1. Circle the correct words to complete the paragraph below.

   The human life cycle begins when an egg is **fertilised** / **pollinated**.

   Next, humans develop into a **sperm** / **foetus**, then a baby

   and then a child. The name given to the stage between childhood

   and adulthood is **adolescence** / **puberty**. After growing into

   an adult, we eventually reach old age, followed by death.

   _____
   3 marks

2. A cuckoo is a type of bird.
   Tick the two stages below that are part of a cuckoo's life cycle.

   [ ] egg   [ ] chrysalis   [ ] piglet   [ ] chick

   _____
   1 mark

3. Look at the gears below and tick the sentence that is correct.

   [ ] Turning gear 1 will turn gear 2
       at the same speed.

   [ ] Turning gear 1 won't turn gear 2.

   [ ] Turning gear 1 will turn gear 2
       in the opposite direction.

   [ ] Turning gear 2 will break gear 1.

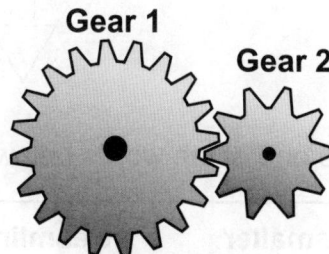

   Gear 1

   Gear 2

   _____
   1 mark

4. The sentences, A-C, describe three new plants.
Put the letter of each sentence in the correct column of the table to
show whether that plant was made by sexual or asexual reproduction.

A This new plant was
grown using cuttings.

B This new plant has two
parent plants.

C This new plant was
made using pollen.

Sexual reproduction	Asexual reproduction

_____
3 marks

5. The picture below shows a skydiver.
The arrows show the two main forces acting on him.

a) Label the forces on the picture.

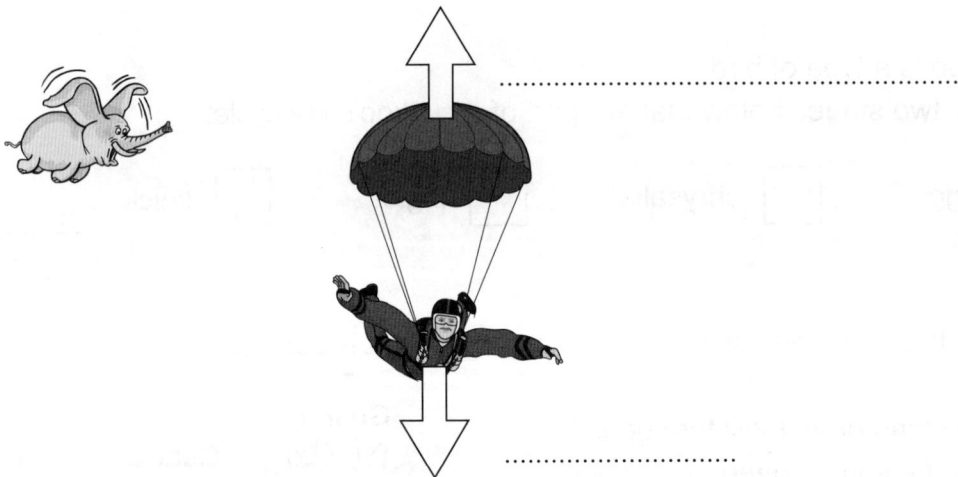

....

....

_____
2 marks

b) Use one of the words below to complete the sentence.

smaller	streamlined	larger	resistance

To fall through the air more slowly, the skydiver would need a

.... parachute.

_____
1 mark

6. Some salt is dissolved in a small pan of water.
Explain how heating the pan over a long period of time
will separate the salt and the water.

....

....

7. Earth is orbited by the moon.

a) Different parts of Earth's moon are lit up at different times of the
month. Which one of these pictures below shows a new moon?
Tick the correct box.

☐   ☐   ☐   ☐

b) What is the length of time between one new moon and the next?

....

c) Explain your answer to (b).

....

....

....

Score: / 16

Test 2 – Graphs, Charts and Tables

1. Zion is investigating the properties of wood and steel.

   a) He finds that steel conducts electricity and wood doesn't.
      What is the only conclusion he can make from these results?

   ☐ All metals conduct electricity.

   ☐ Steel must also conduct heat.

   ☐ Everything apart from wood conducts electricity.

   ☐ Steel is a conductor and wood is an insulator.

   1 mark

   b) Describe a test that Zion could do to find out if wood is magnetic.

   ....

   ....

   1 mark

2. A teacher measures the time it takes for three of her pupils
   to swim across a swimming pool.

   Sam does it in 20 seconds, Parth in 15 seconds and
   Inga in 17 seconds. Add headings to the table below
   and then use the table to record these results.

   3 marks

3. Sugar dissolves in water to make a solution.

a) Piper is told that:

weight of solution = weight of sugar + weight of water

Piper tests this using different amounts of sugar and water.
Complete the table below with the results Piper would expect.
The first column has been done for you.

Weight of sugar (g)	10	55	55	120
Weight of water (g)	100	100	200	300
Weight of solution (g)	110			

2 marks

In a different experiment, Piper records the largest amount of sugar
that will dissolve in 100 g of water at different temperatures.
Her results are shown in the bar chart below.

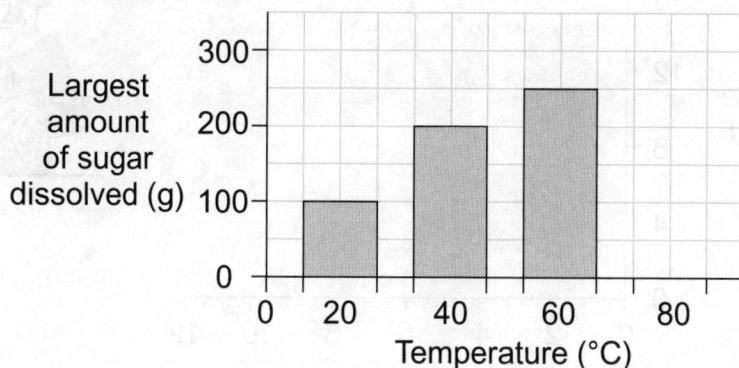

b) At 80 °C, 300 g of sugar dissolved.
Draw this result on the bar chart.

1 mark

c) How many more grams of sugar were
dissolved at 60 °C than at 20 °C?

....

1 mark

4. Shruti attaches a parachute, 4 cm wide, to a ping pong ball.
    She drops the parachute from an upstairs window
    and measures the time it takes to reach the ground.
    She then repeats this with parachutes of different sizes.

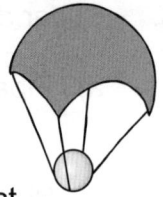

    a) Give one variable that Shruti should control to make this a fair test.

    ....

    1 mark

    Her results from the experiment are shown below.

Parachute width (cm)	4	6	8	10	12
Time it takes the ball to hit the ground (s)	6	10	14	16	18

    b) Plot the results on the scatter graph below.
        The first one has been done for you.

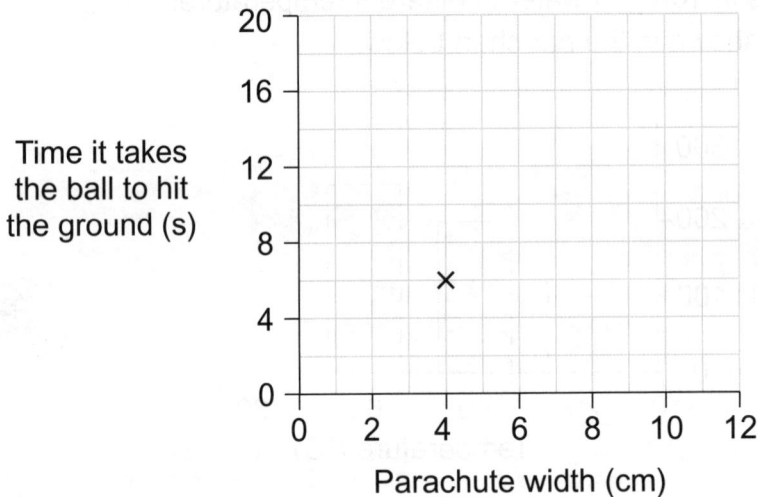

Time it takes
the ball to hit
the ground (s)

Parachute width (cm)

3 marks

    c) Write a conclusion based on Shruti's results.

    ....

    ....

    1 mark

    Score: / 14

Scramble and Search

Unscramble the words below, which all relate to topics in this book. Then find the words in the wordsearch — they can go up, down, forwards or backwards. Hint: The first letter of every scrambled word is the same in the unscrambled word.

PALETN = _ _ _ _ _ _

MONO = _ _ _ _

CISUTNGT = _ _ _ _ _ _ _ _

PURTYEB = _ _ _ _ _ _ _

GATRYIV = _ _ _ _ _ _ _

FCITROIN = _ _ _ _ _ _ _ _

CYRASHILS = _ _ _ _ _ _ _ _ _

TPALOED = _ _ _ _ _ _ _

PELLUY = _ _ _ _ _ _

LEERV = _ _ _ _ _

DLOSVESI = _ _ _ _ _ _ _ _

ANSCOLEDECE = _ _ _ _ _ _ _ _ _ _ _

FENRIGTIL = _ _ _ _ _ _ _ _ _

RIDCOTEROPUN = _ _ _ _ _ _ _ _ _ _ _ _

N	O	I	T	C	U	D	O	R	P	E	R	A	M	P	K	S
I	F	R	I	C	T	I	O	N	P	C	E	E	Y	L	B	G
N	X	D	Z	U	W	C	A	T	U	W	V	M	O	O	P	N
R	L	V	E	A	O	H	F	I	L	T	E	R	I	N	G	I
R	A	T	E	G	E	R	P	E	L	E	L	O	P	D	A	T
P	U	B	E	R	T	Y	A	D	E	R	C	R	F	I	V	T
E	H	F	O	U	W	S	G	I	Y	T	I	V	A	R	G	U
V	I	T	T	E	N	A	L	P	C	S	R	H	H	S	A	C
O	S	V	B	F	D	L	A	E	G	E	C	Y	R	M	S	J
H	S	U	R	Y	D	I	S	S	O	L	V	E	A	O	G	R
D	O	R	Y	J	E	S	F	O	U	B	Z	S	B	O	N	L
T	Q	C	P	W	K	A	D	O	L	E	S	C	E	N	C	E

39

Section 6 — Mixed Practice

Answers

Section 1 – Living Things and Their Habitats

Getting Started – page 2

1. E.g. a pond

2. a) by insects
by wind

   b) E.g. seeds are carried away from the parent plant.

3.

Test 1 – Life Cycles – pages 3-5

1.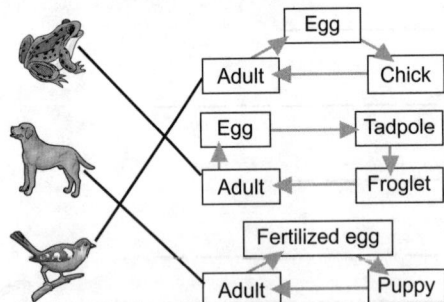

(2 marks for all correct, otherwise 1 mark for one correct)

2. The following sentences should be ticked: Female mammals usually carry their developing offspring inside themselves. Most female mammals give birth to live young. (1 mark for each)

3. a)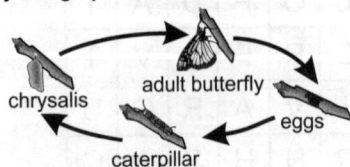

(1 mark for each)

   b) E.g. birds don't have a chrysalis stage in their life cycle. (1 mark)

   c) E.g. both hatch from eggs. (1 mark)

4. a) amphibians, insects and birds (1 mark, can be in any order)

   b) amphibians (1 mark)

   c) insects (1 mark)

5.

Name of animal	Does it lay eggs?	Name of its young	What type of animal is it?
Aha ha	Yes	larva	insect
Kagu	Yes	chick	bird
Golden Mantella	Yes	tadpole	amphibian
Fossa	No	cub	mammal

(3 marks for all correct, otherwise 2 marks for two or three correct or 1 mark for one correct)

Test 2 – Reproduction – pages 6-8

1. a) A male and a female lion (1 mark)

   b) E.g. to sexually reproduce there needs to be a sperm from an adult male and an egg from an adult female. (1 mark)

2. Some plants can reproduce without being **pollinated**. **Asexual** reproduction is when a new plant grows from small **cuttings** of an old plant. Growing plants, such as daffodils, from **bulbs** is also asexual reproduction. (3 marks for all correct, otherwise 2 marks for two or three correct or 1 mark for one correct)

3. a)

(1 mark for all circles correct, 1 mark for all crosses correct)

   b) The fertilised egg develops into an embryo. — 3
   The sperm joins with the egg, fertilising it. — 2
   The embryo continues to grow into a baby animal. — 4
   The sperm swims towards the egg. — 1
   (2 marks for all correct, otherwise 1 mark for one correct)

Answers

4. a)

anther — stigma
filament — style
petal — ovary

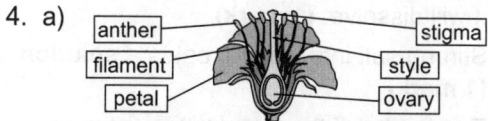

**(4 marks for all correct, otherwise
3 marks for four or five correct,
2 marks for two or three correct or
1 mark for one correct)**

b) Pollination happens when **pollen**
from one plant lands on the **stigma** of
another plant. Fertilisation happens
after pollination. This is when the pollen
grain and the **egg** join and this develops
into a **seed**. **(3 marks for all correct,
otherwise 2 marks for two or three
correct or 1 mark for one correct)**

Living Things Thinker – page 9

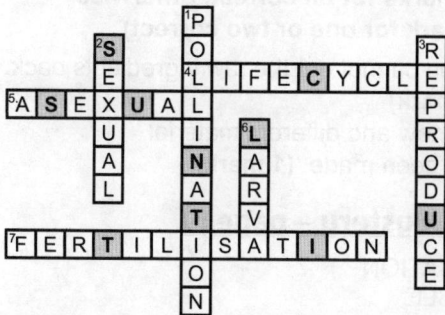

Asexual reproduction happens in plants when
BULBS or CUTTINGS are planted in damp soil.

Section 2 – Animals Including Humans

Getting Started – page 10

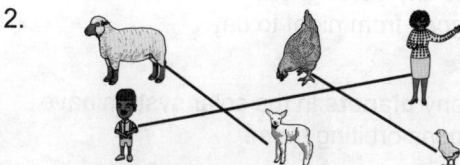

1.

2   1   3

2.

3. My teacher is **an adult**.

Test 1 – Human Growth – pages 11-13

1. The following sentences should be circled:
Elephants are pregnant for more than a
year longer than humans. **(1 mark)**
The gestation period of a human is
9 months. **(1 mark)**

2. True **(1 mark)**, true **(1 mark)**,
false **(1 mark)**, false **(1 mark)**

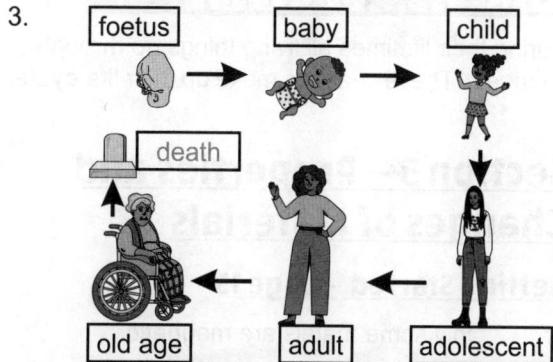

3.

foetus   baby   child
death
old age   adult   adolescent

**(4 marks for all correct, otherwise
3 marks for four or five correct,
2 marks for two or three correct or
1 mark for one correct)**

4. a)

Changes	Boys	Girls
Their testicles begin to produce sperm.	✓	✗
Their hips become wider.	✗	✓
More oil is produced in their skin.	✓	✓
Their voices become deeper.	✓	✗
Hair starts to grow on their bodies.	✓	✓

(1 mark for each correct row)

b) E.g. their periods begin / they begin to
develop breasts / they experience mood
swings. **(2 marks for two correct answers
or 1 mark for one correct answer)**

Answers

Unscramble to Escape – page 14

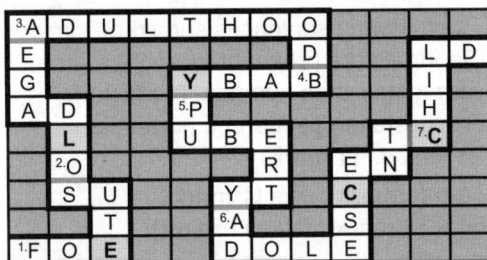

³·A	D	U	L	T	H	O	O					
E						D				L	D	
G				Y	B	A	⁴·B			I		
A	D		⁵·P							H		
	L			U	B	E			T	⁷·C		
	²·O				R		E	N				
	S	U		Y	T		C					
	T				⁶·A		S					
¹·F	O	E		D	O	L	E					

During their lifetimes all living things go through changes. These changes make up their life **cycle**.

Section 3 – Properties and Changes of Materials

Getting Started – page 15

1. Only some metals are magnetic.

2.

melting → evaporating

ice → water → steam

freezing ← condensing

3. Electric wires are made from copper and are covered with plastic. Copper is a **good** electrical conductor. Electricity can flow through it with **ease**. Plastic is a **good** electrical insulator, so it protects you from getting an electric shock.

Test 1 – Material Properties and Changes – pages 16-18

1. a) plastic sandwich bag **(1 mark)**
    b) steel screw and wooden table **(1 mark)**
    c) plastic sandwich bag and wooden table **(1 mark)**

2.

sand and water — small-holed sieve

sand and iron filings — medium-holed sieve

flour and rice — filter paper

marbles and sand — magnet

(2 marks for all correct, otherwise 1 mark for at least one correct)

3. a) It will dissolve. **(1 mark)**
    b) Stirring salt into water creates a **solution. (1 mark)**
    c) Evaporate off the water to leave the salt behind. **(1 mark)**

4. a) aluminium foil **(1 mark)**
    b) E.g. because it was the best thermal insulator tested **(1 mark)**, so it would help to keep a drink hot for longer than the other materials would **(1 mark)**.

5. a) E.g. a reversible change is a change that can be undone / a change where you can get the original materials back **(1 mark)**.
    b) melting an ice cube,
        dissolving sugar in water,
        mixing flour and salt
        (2 marks for all correct, otherwise 1 mark for one or two correct)
    c) ...you cannot get the raw ingredients back. **(1 mark)**
        ...a new and different material has been made. **(1 mark)**

Material Mystery – page 19

CONDENSATION
REVERSIBLE
FILTERING
SOLUTION
MIXTURE
SOLUBLE
Mystery word: IRREVERSIBLE

Section 4 – Earth and Space

Getting Started – page 20

1. Jupiter, Neptune and the Earth should be circled.

2. The following sentences should be ticked:
    The sky gets lighter.
    It goes from night to day.

3. a) one
    b) Many **planets** in the solar system have moons orbiting them.

Answers

Test 1 – The Sun, Planets and Moon – pages 21-23

1.

The Sun | day time | Earth | night time

(1 mark for both labels correct)

2. The Sun **(1 mark)**

3. As the day goes on, the Sun appears to move across the sky from **East** to **West**. This happens because the Earth is **rotating**.
(1 mark for each correct word)

4. a)

Distance from the Sun

Mercury
Venus
Earth
Mars
Jupiter
Saturn
Uranus
Neptune

(1 mark for each planet in the correct position)

b) gravity / the Sun's gravitational pull **(1 mark)**

c) spherical **(1 mark)**

5. False **(1 mark)**

6. How long the Earth takes to rotate once on its axis = 24 hours **(1 mark)**
How long it takes the Moon to orbit the Earth = 28 days **(1 mark)**
How long it takes the Earth to orbit the Sun = 365 days **(1 mark)**

7. a) B **(1 mark)**

b) E.g. because the side of the Moon facing the Earth has no sunlight on it / isn't reflecting any sunlight **(1 mark)**.

Solar System Search – page 24

MOON
GRAVITY
ROTATES
DAYTIME
SPHERE
SUN
PLANETS
Missing planet — JUPITER

Section 5 – Forces

Getting Started – page 25

1. These three should be circled:
A woman using a force to kick a football.
A karate champion using a force to break a block.
A boy using a force to pull a sledge of gifts across snow.

2. The bottom of an ice skate should be made of **polished metal**.
A cycle path should be made of **fairly smooth pavement**.

Test 1 – Forces – pages 26-28

1. Forces are always **pushes** or **pulls (1 mark)**.
It's easier to pull an object across a **smooth** surface than a **rough** surface **(1 mark)**.
It's easier for a person to walk through **air** than **water (1 mark)**.

2. slow down, speed up, speed up, slow down
(2 marks for all correct, otherwise 1 mark for at least one correct)

3. Skis sliding on snow —————— As little friction as possible
Car tyres rolling on a road — As much friction as possible
Holding onto a rock when rock climbing — Some friction, but not too much
(2 marks for all lines correct, otherwise 1 mark for one line correct)

4. a) A force that pulls all objects towards the Earth's centre **(1 mark)**.

b)

(1 mark for each arrow)

5. a) Air resistance **(1 mark)** and water resistance **(1 mark)**

b)

The car has a smooth/rounded/low to the ground/flat shape **(1 mark)**.

Answers

Answers

c) The dolphin should be circled.
It can swim faster **(1 mark)** as it has low water resistance **(1 mark)**.

Test 2 – Levers, Pulleys and Gears – pages 29-31

1. pulley **(1 mark)**
lever **(1 mark)**

2. B, A, C, D **(2 marks for all in the correct place, otherwise 1 mark for two in the correct place)**

3. The fishing rod, bottle opener, nutcracker and crane should be circled. **(1 mark for each correctly circled object)**

4. a) Method 2 **(1 mark)**
b) Move the pivot closer to the bag / make the pole on his side of the pivot longer **(1 mark)**.

5. Clocks use **gears** to turn the hour, minute and second hands. The **cogs** connected to each hand have a different number of **teeth**, so they turn **at different speeds**. **(2 marks for all words correct, otherwise 1 mark for two words correct)**

6. a) removing a nail **(1 mark)**
b) A small force is applied to the end of the hammer's handle at a large distance from the pivot **(1 mark)**. A large force is produced and applied to the nail by the hammer's claw, which is much closer to the pivot **(1 mark)**.

Mechanisms Riddles – page 32

1. scissors, levers
2. a clock, gears
3. a crane, pulleys
4. a seesaw, levers

Section 6 – Mixed Practice

Test 1 – Mixed Test – pages 33-35

1. The human life cycle begins when an egg is **fertilised**. Next, humans develop into a **foetus**, then a baby and then a child. The name given to the stage between childhood and adulthood is **adolescence**. After growing into an adult, we eventually reach old age, followed by death. **(1 mark for each correct word)**

2. egg, chick **(1 mark for both)**

3. Turning gear 1 will turn gear 2 in the opposite direction **(1 mark)**.

4.
Sexual reproduction	Asexual reproduction
B C	A

(1 mark for each letter in the correct column)

5. a)

air resistance

gravity

(1 mark for each correct label)

b) To fall through the air more slowly, the skydiver would need a **larger** parachute. **(1 mark)**

6. E.g. the water will evaporate and the salt will be left behind in the pan **(1 mark)**.

7. a)

(1 mark)

b) 28 days **(1 mark)**

c) E.g. the Moon takes 28 days to complete one full orbit of Earth **(1 mark)**, so it takes 28 days for the next new moon / for the Moon to be back in this same position **(1 mark)**.

Answers

Test 2 – Graphs, Charts and Tables – pages 36-38

1. a) Steel is a conductor and wood is an insulator **(1 mark)**.

   b) E.g. move wood closer and closer to a magnet and see if it is attracted to the magnet **(1 mark for any suitable test idea)**.

2. E.g.

Pupil	Time (seconds)
Sam	20
Parth	15
Inga	17

(1 mark for correct headings, 1 mark for one pupil and their time recorded correctly, 1 mark for all three pupils and their times recorded correctly)

3. a)

Weight of sugar (g)	10	55	55	120
Weight of water (g)	100	100	200	300
Weight of solution (g)	110	155	255	420

(2 marks for all correct, otherwise 1 mark for one or two correct)

   b)

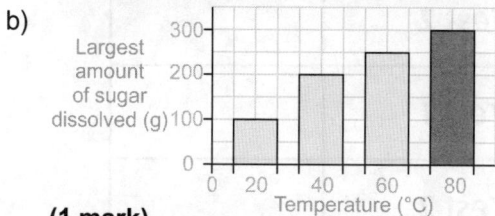

(1 mark)

   c) 150 g **(1 mark)**

4. a) E.g. she should use the same ball / use parachutes of the same material / drop the ball from the same point / make sure the weather conditions are the same for all drops **(1 mark)**.

   b)

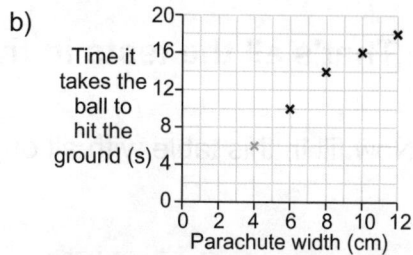

(3 marks for all points plotted correctly, otherwise 2 marks for two or three points plotted correctly or 1 mark for one point plotted correctly)

   c) E.g. the larger the parachute width, the longer the ball takes to hit the ground **(1 mark)**.

Scramble and Search – page 39

PALETN = planet

CISUTNGT = cuttings

GATRYIV = gravity

CYRASHILS = chrysalis

PELLUY = pulley

MONO = moon

PURTYEB = puberty

FCITROIN = friction

TPALOED = tadpole

LEERV = lever

DLOSVESI = dissolve

ANSCOLEDECE = adolescence

FENRIGTIL = filtering

RIDCOTEROPUN = reproduction

N	O	I	T	C	U	D	O	R	P	E	R	A	M	P	K	S
I	F	R	I	C	T	I	O	N	P	C	E	E	Y	L	B	G
N	X	D	Z	U	W	C	A	T	U	W	V	M	O	O	P	N
R	L	V	E	A	O	H	F	I	L	T	E	R	I	N	G	I
R	A	T	E	G	E	R	P	E	L	E	L	O	P	D	A	T
P	U	B	E	R	T	Y	A	D	E	R	C	R	F	I	V	T
E	H	F	O	U	W	S	G	I	Y	T	I	V	A	R	G	U
V	I	T	T	E	N	A	L	P	C	S	R	H	H	S	A	C
O	S	V	B	F	D	L	A	E	G	E	C	Y	R	M	S	J
H	S	U	R	Y	D	I	S	S	O	L	V	E	A	O	G	R
D	O	R	Y	J	E	S	F	O	U	B	Z	S	B	O	N	L
T	Q	C	P	W	K	A	D	O	L	E	S	C	E	N	C	E

45

Progress Chart

That's all the tests in the book done — great job!

Now fill in this table with all of your scores and see how you got on.

		Score
Living Things and Their Habitats	Test 1	
	Test 2	
Animals Including Humans	Test 1	
Properties and Changes of Materials	Test 1	
Earth and Space	Test 1	
Forces	Test 1	
	Test 2	
Mixed Practice	Test 1	
	Test 2	

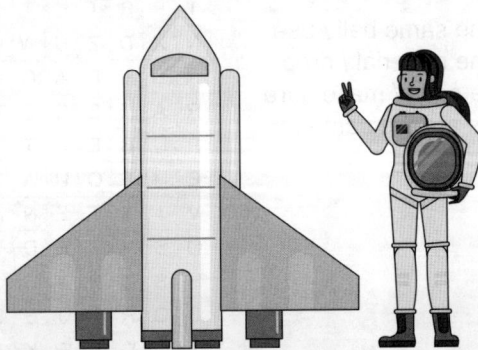

This page may be photocopied